Changes

Written by Joanne Jessop

Wayland

Boxes   Light
Changes   Patterns
Holes   Textures
Journeys   Wheels

Picture acknowledgements

The publishers would like to thank the following for allowing their photographs to be reproduced in this book: Cephas 6, 14, 15; Bruce Coleman Ltd 7 (above) Hans Reinhard (below) Jane Burton, 8 (both) Jane Burton, 9 (both) Jane Burton, 10 (main picture) Dr Eckart Pott (inset) Erwin and Peggy Bauer, 11 O. Langrand, 12 and 13 Kim Taylor, 16 (both) Jane Burton, 17 George McCarthy, 19 Michael Freeman, 21 Michael Freeman; Chris Fairclough 4, 5, 22, 23, 25, 26 (both), 27 (both); *cover* Zul Mukhida; Oxford Scientific Films Ltd *title page* Rudie H. Kuiter; Popperfoto 28; Topham Picture Library 30; Wayland Picture Library 18, 20 (both); Tim Woodcock/TWP 29.

Cover photography by Zul Mukhida, organized by Zoe Hargreaves. With thanks to Stanford Infants School. A special thank you to Imogen and Conrad.

First published in 1992 by
Wayland (Publishers) Ltd
61 Western Road, Hove
East Sussex BN3 1JD, England

Editor: Francesca Motisi
Designers: Jean and Robert Wheeler

Consultant: Alison Watkins is an experienced teacher with a special interest in language and reading. She has been a class teacher but at present is the special needs coordinator for a school in Hackney. Alison wrote the notes for parents and teachers and provided the topic web.

British Library Cataloguing in Publication Data

Jessop, Joanne
Changes. – (Criss cross)
I. Title II. Series
155.4

ISBN 0-7502-0353-6

Typeset by DJS Fotoset Ltd, Brighton, Sussex
Printed and bound in Italy by L.E.G.O. S.p.A., Vicenza

Contents

The answers to the questions in the text can be found on page 32. Words that appear in **bold** in the text are explained in the glossary on page 32.

Everything changes

day

Everything around us changes. The weather changes; the seasons change. Children grow and change into adults. Day changes into night.

night

These pictures show a city street during the day and at night. Many changes have happened. What changes can you find?

Changes in nature

The seasons change through the year. In spring new life begins. Spring changes into warm summer months. This is a time of growth.

Then autumn arrives and the leaves change colour. Autumn is followed by winter.

Snow covers the ground, and all of nature is at rest, waiting for spring to come again.

As the seasons change, the colours of nature also change. These pictures show a leaf changing from its summer colour to its autumn colour.

The leaf changes
from green to a
bronze colour and
finally to red.

Camouflage

Some animals change colour to blend in with their surroundings. This is good **camouflage**. When the winter snow starts to fall, the arctic fox's coat changes from brown to white.

A chameleon changes colour to match its background. When a chameleon sits in a tree, it turns green so that it can hide among the leaves.

Growth

As a seed grows,
it changes into
a plant.

The runner bean in these
pictures sends out tiny
roots and leaves. The
roots grow deeper and
the leaves get bigger
as the seed changes into
a plant.

This lamb will grow bigger and
change into a sheep.

This month-old calf will grow
into a big cow, like its mum!

Metamorphosis

Some animals change from one form into another as they grow. This is called **metamorphosis.**

A tiny tadpole hatches out of **frogspawn** in a pond. As the tadpole gets bigger, it grows legs and its tail disappears. After several weeks, the tadpole has changed into a frog.

Changes in people

Our feelings and moods change.
Sometimes we are happy and smiling;
at other times we are sad and feel like
crying. Some days we may want to
be quiet; other days we may want to
shout and run about.

Getting older

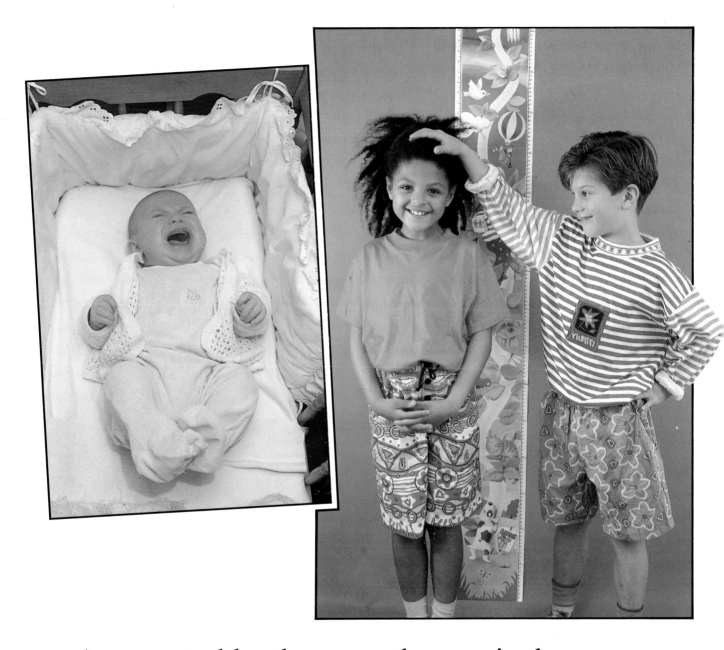

As we get older there are changes in the way we look and the things we can do. A baby gets bigger and begins to walk and talk. Children grow taller and learn more at school.

A child gets older and becomes an adult. The
boy in this picture is listening to his grand-
father's stories of life when he was young.
What changes do you think his grandfather
might be talking about?

Changing clothes

We change our clothes many times. We put on
warm clothes when we play outside in winter.
These children are wearing clothes that keep
them warm and dry in the snow.

When the weather gets warmer, we wear different clothes. Shorts and T-shirts keep us cool in summer. What are some other reasons for changing our clothes?

Changes in our world

The world around us is always changing.
Fashions in clothing change over the years.
What your parents wore when they were children
may seem old-fashioned today.

These pictures show children in the 1950s and children today. What changes can you see?

Changes by cooking

Food is changed when it is cooked. Cakes look very different after they are baked.

26

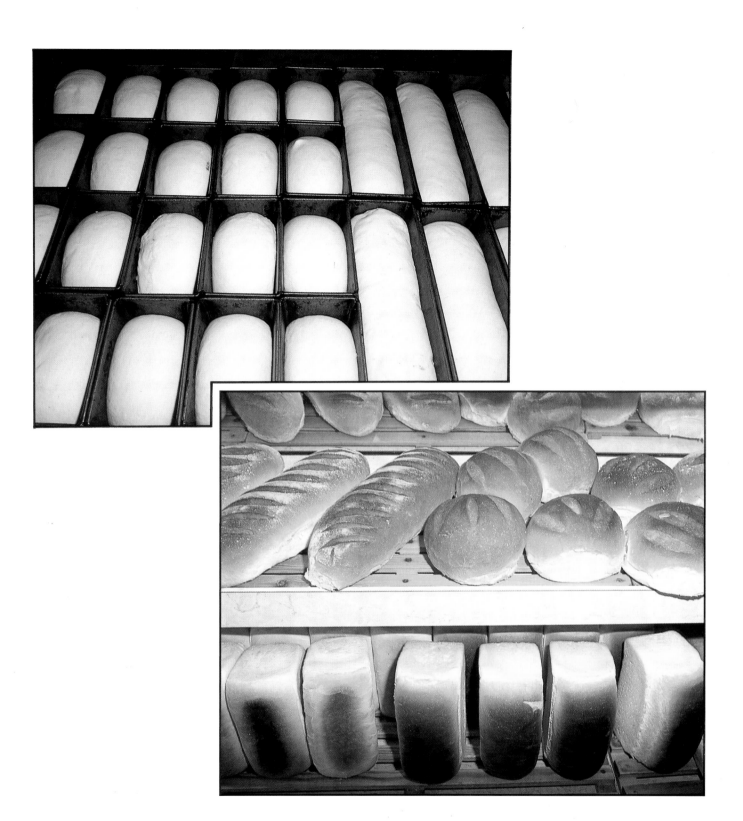

These pans of dough were changed into loaves of bread when they were baked in an oven.

Changes in technology

Technology is changed and improved when scientists make new **discoveries**. The first televisions were large and bulky, and the picture was only in black and white.

Now we have colour TV and video recorders. We can even use televisions to play computer games. Think of some other changes in technology we may have in the future.

Notes for parents and teachers

Maths
- Use real life situations e.g. shop, bank, café, travel agent, for the children to deal with money. This could be set up in the home corner.
- Investigate ways of changing numbers through number operations and using number machines.

Language
- The theme 'Changes' can lead to a wide range of writing activities: diary writing, lists of changes, story writing, brainstorming ideas and making notes, scientific writing e.g. life history of the frog , making books, poetry writing (words to express mood changes and emotions).
- By interviewing grandparents about the past, the children are developing their interviewing, questioning and listening skills. The interview could be taped and relevant quotes or sections could be written in the appropriate form.
- Children could develop their research and library skills by using non-fiction books to find out about the past.
- Children could learn how writing has evolved and the development and use of the modern word-processor. (Did their parents or grandparents have computers when they were at school?)

History
- A wealth of historical concepts and activities will naturally arise from this theme. Teachers/parents could investigate change depending on the interest of the child/children, e.g. toys, transport, clothes and fashion, schools, etc . . .
- Time lines could be put up in the classroom relevant to the focus (e.g. human growth could be represented by pegging up baby clothes → adult clothes).
- Use of artefacts, visits and first-hand experience is necessary to aid children's understanding of change (e.g. photographs, museums, documents, etc).

Science and Technology
- Use fiction books to reinforce or introduce scientific concepts of growth, change and metamorphosis.
- Children can design and make weather instruments to detect changes in the weather (e.g. weather vanes).
- Changes in the growth of plants can be recorded by close observation drawings, keeping a diary, or taking photographs.

Geography
- Changes in the local environment is a first hand way of understanding change. Use photographs, visits, interview parents/grandparents, local shopkeepers, etc.
- Children could be made aware of the factors affecting the changing environment and the human influence on the earth (e.g. pollution, deforestation, tourism, population changes etc.). Drama and fiction would be suitable media to use for young children.
- Changes in scenery/environment (e.g. going on holiday from the city to the country or seaside).

Art/Craft
- Effective pictures could be created by children exploring the idea of camouflage. This could be represented in 2D or 3D form.

Personal and Social Education
- We change clothes for many reasons. Some reasons are shown in the book, but we also change our clothes for personal hygiene and cleanliness.
- Card picture games (or language games) such as 'pairs' or 'snap', would help children match the appropriate clothing to the appropriate occasion or weather.
- Changes occur in our lives. Moving house, starting a new school, being ill (and then well again). Also, changes can occur in our family structure (e.g. older brothers and sisters moving away, someone coming to stay, separation of parents, death in the family, etc.).

Music
- Children could interview their parent/s about the type of music they enjoyed when they were younger and how music has changed.

Dance/Drama/PE
- Children can explore ways of changing their body shape and their expressions and feelings. They could be encouraged to see that they have control over their own body movements. Their self-image and confidence would also be enhanced.

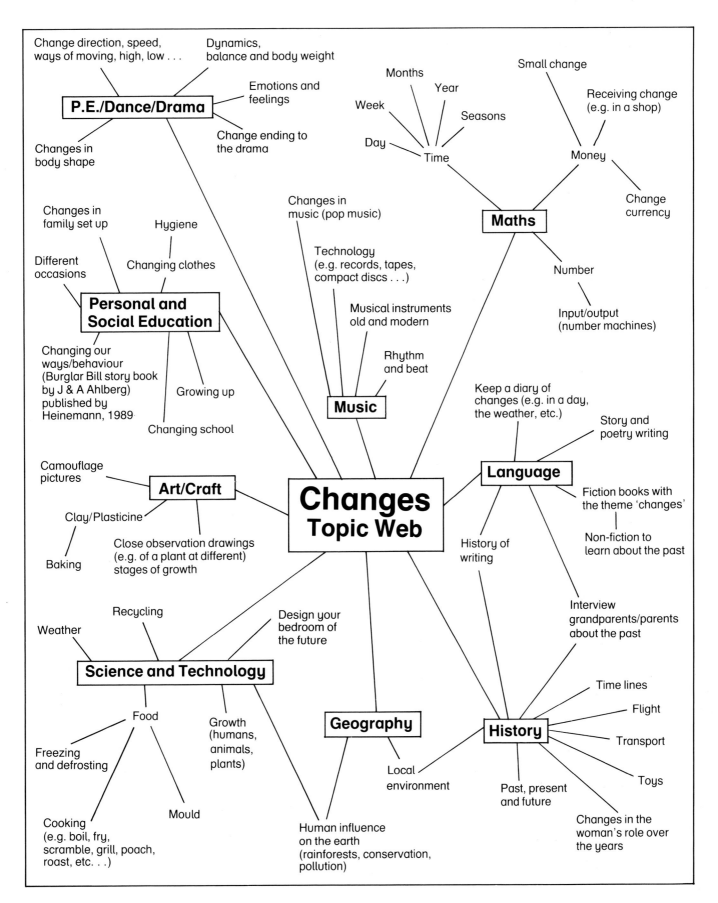

Change direction, speed, ways of moving, high, low . . .

Dynamics, balance and body weight

Emotions and feelings

P.E./Dance/Drama

Changes in body shape

Change ending to the drama

Changes in family set up

Hygiene

Different occasions

Changing clothes

Personal and Social Education

Changing our ways/behaviour (Burglar Bill story book by J & A Ahlberg) published by Heinemann, 1989

Growing up

Changing school

Camouflage pictures

Art/Craft

Clay/Plasticine

Baking

Close observation drawings (e.g. of a plant at different) stages of growth

Changes in music (pop music)

Technology (e.g. records, tapes, compact discs . . .)

Musical instruments old and modern

Rhythm and beat

Music

Months

Year

Week

Seasons

Day

Time

Small change

Receiving change (e.g. in a shop)

Money

Change currency

Maths

Number

Input/output (number machines)

Keep a diary of changes (e.g. in a day, the weather, etc.)

Story and poetry writing

Language

Fiction books with the theme 'changes'

Non-fiction to learn about the past

History of writing

Interview grandparents/parents about the past

Changes
Topic Web

Recycling

Weather

Design your bedroom of the future

Science and Technology

Food

Growth (humans, animals, plants)

Freezing and defrosting

Geography

Cooking (e.g. boil, fry, scramble, grill, poach, roast, etc. . .)

Mould

Local environment

Human influence on the earth (rainforests, conservation, pollution)

History

Time lines

Flight

Transport

Toys

Past, present and future

Changes in the woman's role over the years

Glossary

Camouflage   An animal's shape or colour that makes it look like its natural surroundings.

Discoveries   Things and ideas that are thought of for the first time.

Fashions   The current style, or way of dressing.

Frogspawn   The mass of eggs produced by a frog.

Metamorphosis   The changes in form that certain animals go through as they grow and develop.

Technology   The things that are made to change the world around us, and to meet our needs. Television is an example.

Answers

Pages 4/5 The sun has set and it is now dark. The people have gone home and electric lights have been switched on. The time on the clock has changed.

Page 23 Other reasons for changing our clothes may be for a special occasion like a wedding, or for cleanliness.

Pages 24/25 The children's clothes on page 25 are much more casual. They are wearing T-shirts, shorts, track-suits and trainers.

Index